This journal belongs to

_____

_____

Date

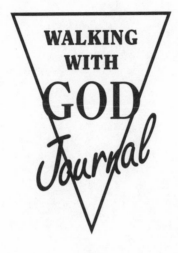

WALKING
WITH
GOD
Journal

Zondervan PublishingHouse
Grand Rapids, Michigan

A Division of HarperCollins*Publishers*

Walking With God Journal

Copyright ©1992 by Willow Creek Community Church
All rights reserved

Published by Zondervan Publishing House
Grand Rapids, Michigan 49530

Produced by The Livingstone Corporation. James C. Galvin,
J. Michael Kendrick, and Daryl J. Lucas, editors.

ISBN 0-310-91642-9

Cover design: Cindy Davis
Interior design: Catherine Bergstrom

Printed in the United States of America

92 93 94 95 96 97 98   99
9   8   7   6   5   4   3   2   1

How to Use This Journal

A vital part of every believer's spiritual life is the time spent alone with God and his Word. The *Walking With God Journal* is the perfect companion to a quiet time with God.

Considering the pace of life, it's often difficult for the average person to keep regular appointments with God when the demands of earning a living, raising a family, participating in church life, and building relationships with others are so great. With these concerns in mind, we designed this basic journal to encourage you in your spiritual journey.

No two people take the same amount of space when writing, so the blank pages allow you the flexibility of using one page each day or as many as you need on your walk with God. The *Walking With God Journal* can be used to keep your notes during Bible study, record your prayers, or simply jot down your thoughts and ideas. Using the *Walking With God Journal* will help you maintain a vital connection with God.

How to Have a Quiet Time

You Are What You Eat is the title of a popular book that explains how your physical health is a product of your diet. The better the nutritional intake, the healthier the individual. The same principle applies to your spiritual life as well. A key to "eating right" spiritually is spending time alone with Christ.

Jesus said, "Remain in me, and I will remain in you. No branch can bear fruit by itself; it must remain in the vine. Neither can you bear fruit unless you remain in me. I am the vine; you are the branches. If a man remains in me and I in him, he will bear much fruit; apart from me you can do nothing" (John 15:4-5). But practically speaking, how do we "remain in Christ"? How does a Christian eat the right spiritual foods?

The source of this nutrition is fellowship with Jesus, commonly referred to as a quiet time. Simply defined, a quiet time is unhurried time alone with God consisting of Bible study and prayer. Despite the simplicity of this definition, you may ask, "When I have these times with the Lord, how do I know I'm doing the right thing?" To answer this question, many believers have come up with formulas for the perfect quiet time and insist that if these methods are not followed to the letter, the quiet time "doesn't count." Of course, there is no single method that is better than another. The best way to view your appointment with God is as a special time to develop your relationship, much as two close friends or a husband and wife strive to spend meaningful, uninterrupted time together.

Try to keep the proper perspective as you establish a consistent quiet time. Do everything you can to prevent this time from becoming cold or legalistic. You're developing a deep friendship with the Living God, so don't mindlessly recite pat phrases or prayers. Don't feel you have to follow a specific routine every single day in order to somehow gain God's favor. Disciplining yourself to spend time with Jesus is commendable, but beware of this habit turning into a lifeless routine.

Setting Aside the Time

It may be helpful for some people to have a special time in the day and a specific place in their home or office that is set aside for their time with the Lord. Others may not be able to enjoy a set routine and will opt for a variety of times and places. Regardless of the schedule you choose, be sure to have a plan that ensures you do meet with God. For example, some prefer to have quiet times first thing in the morning, while others favor evening hours. Neither is better—it just depends on what works for you. We would suggest sharing your plan with a friend who can encourage you to stick to it.

Some Creative Ideas for Quiet Times

1. Listen to a praise tape (or other tape featuring worshipful music).
2. Take a walk outside or a ride in the country, praising God for the beauty you see around you.
3. Vary your scheduled time with the Lord by praying only, by studying the Bible only, by meditating on God's qualities, and so on.

A.C.T.S.—A Pattern for Prayer

There are many ways to bring creativity and discipline into your prayer life, and the A.C.T.S. pattern of prayer is one that you might find helpful. A.C.T.S. stands for:

A **Adoration** *(see Psalm 100)*
Adoration is personal worship of God. We describe God out loud, we worship and adore him, and we tell him what we think of him. It differs from thanksgiving in that we are praising God for who he is rather than for what he's done.

C **Confession** *(see 1 John 1:9; Psalm 139:23-24)*

When we confess our sins to God, we don't inform God of anything—he already knows what we've done. Rather, we are telling God that we agree with his assessment of our thoughts and deeds.

T **Thanksgiving** *(see 1 Thessalonians 5:16-18; Luke 17:11-18)*

Thanksgiving is the expression of our pleasure and gratitude for what God has done for us. Because he has made all things and has looked after our needs, he is worthy of our thanks.

S **Supplication** *(see Philippians 4:6-7; 1 John 5:14-15)*

In supplication, we ask for God's intervention in our lives, most significantly where resistance to his plans and purposes is greatest. We give him an opportunity to perform his will. And most important, we let our needs—personal, corporate, and even global—be made known to Someone who can and will help.

Some Creative Ideas for Prayer

1. Write out your prayers in longhand, like a letter to a friend.
2. In the front of your journal, write out a list of various topics to pray about. Assign days of the week for each topic.
3. Vary the A.C.T.S. pattern: spend one day entirely in adoration, another entirely in confession, and so on.

Remember, prayer is a spiritual lifeline that acknowledges God's presence and secures God's power for our daily lives. Therefore, "pray continually" (1 Thessalonians 5:17).

B.R.O.A.M.—A Simple Outline for Bible Study

If you want to study the Bible more deeply, you may find an inductive Bible study helpful. The approach called B.R.O.A.M. has five steps.

Step 1: Background

Choose a book of the Bible and familiarize yourself with its background. The questions you ask are those of a good reporter:

- Who wrote the book (or letter)?
- To whom was it written?
- What were the circumstances surrounding its writing?
- Why was it written?
- What main themes is the writer emphasizing?

Very often, once you know the answer to these background questions, your study will come alive. Knowing the background can also help you guard against erroneous interpretations because you have a better grasp on the intent of the biblical author.

Note: Any commentary, Bible dictionary, or study Bible contains this information. Books like these are a lifetime investment in your spiritual growth and are well worth owning.

Step 2: Read

During several of your appointments with God, simply read through several chapters or the entire book. Enjoy it! Don't read for any profound insight or deep truths. Just get a feel for what is being said. Try using several translations. After three or four readings, write out a sentence summary of the author's overall message and objective. Underline some of the key verses which support that message.

Note: With shorter books (1 John, for example), one sitting is enough to read the whole book. With larger books, (the Gospels, Psalms, Proverbs, and so on) you will need to break up the reading into manageable portions. In some cases, major themes will be logical breaking points; in others, you can subdivide the reading in order to study the main characters in the book. For instance, you might want to study Genesis by reading the chapters about Abraham one day, those about Isaac the next, and so on.

Step 3: Observe ("What does it mean?")

After several readings, break the book or letter into major ideas or themes. Ask yourself, What is the author saying to his audience? At this stage, do not rely on outlines provided in study Bibles. Come up with your own main divisions and simply write down in your own words what that section is saying. For a longer book, you can go back and expand on your observations during a second or third time through.

Closely related to observation is interpretation—the understanding of nuances, the discernment of subtle shades of meaning, and the correlation of other biblical truths with the observations made. Keep in mind that an interpretation without careful observation easily leads to misinterpretation. As you're writing out your observations, make sure you're accurately noting only what is actually there in Scripture. Be wary of fanciful ideas or impressions—especially mystical "revelations" as if from God—without support from the text itself. Also, you may want to consult a commentary or two to check your findings with what others have observed.

Step 4: Apply ("What should I do?")

We distinguish between observing and applying because often people jump to "what it says to me" instead of carefully understanding the original context of the biblical message. Of course, a person reading the Bible can go to the other extreme—after all, what good is accumulated biblical knowledge if it has no effect on that person's life? After careful observations have been made, the next step is to reflect prayerfully on the text and make specific applications. These applications can relate to any part of your life: home, family, work, church, friends, money, and so on. When you pray to God about how to apply a passage you can be confident it is a prayer he is very interested in answering (see James 1:22; Isaiah 66:2; Hebrews 4:2).

Here are examples of application questions that you can use:
- Is there a promise to claim?
- Is there a command to obey?
- Is there sin to confess?
- Is there an example to follow?
- Is there a behavior to change?
- Is there an encouragement to receive?
- Is there an insight to gain?
- Is there an issue to pray about?
- Is there a reason to worship God?

Step 5: Memorize
The final step in personal Bible study is one of the most far-reaching and long-lasting. By actually memorizing portions of Scripture, you will have truths readily available from God's Word for the Holy Spirit to use in times of need. An added benefit to memorization is that your mind becomes occupied with positive and enriching thoughts. Choose key verses from the book that encapsulate truths worth remembering, and hide those truths in your heart (Psalm 119:11) through memorization.

Now that you have these steps in mind, note that the two key steps are observing and applying; they are at the heart of Bible study.

Some Creative Ideas for Bible Study
1. Read a book of the Bible to study a specific topic, character trait, or Bible character.
2. Meditate on a passage by creating vivid mental pictures of the story or event.
3. Ask questions as you read: What were the people feeling or thinking at that time? What difference does the knowledge of this story make in my life? and so on.

The *Walking With God Journal* can also be used to accompany each of the titles in the *Walking With God Series.* Written by Don Cousins and Judson Poling of the Willow Creek Community Church, these six volumes provide step-by-step instruction for bringing small groups to spiritual maturity.

Titles in this series include:

Friendship With God: Developing Intimacy With God
This study guide leads you to a fresh discovery of the God who loves you, who sought you out, and who desires to know you better as a true friend. (0-310-59143-0)

The Incomparable Jesus: Experiencing the Power of Christ
This study guide will deepen your knowledge and experience of the matchless Forgiver and King named Jesus. (0-310-59153-8)

"Follow Me!": Walking With Jesus in Everyday Life
How does following Jesus affect our relationships, our work, and our finances? This study guide will show you how to obey Jesus' command in everyday life. (0-310-59163-5)

Discovering the Church: Becoming Part of God's New Community
This study guide explores the wonder and beauty of God's plan to connect his children in the life-sustaining community called the church. (0-310-59193-7)

Building Your Church: Using Your Gifts, Time, and Resources
This study guide will help you find your niche in the church so you can truly make a difference. (0-310-59183-X)

Impacting Your World: Becoming a Person of Influence
This study guide will help you determine the style of evangelism that best fits you and gives you practical ways to share your story—and his story—with others. (0-310-59193-7)